The Royal Commission on
Historical Manuscripts

Record Repositories
in Great Britain

A geographical directory

LONDON: HMSO

© Crown copyright 1991

Applications for reproduction should be made to HMSO

First published 1964

Ninth edition 1991

Second impression (with revisions) 1992

ISBN 0 11 440243 4

Cover

The cover illustration shows the search room at Clwyd Record Office, Hawarden. It is reproduced by kind permission of the County Archivist.

Contents

Introduction

Record Repositories sets out to list those institutions in the United Kingdom whose objectives include the systematic collection and preservation of written records other than those of their own administration and which also make regular provision for their public use.

The institutions concerned fall into four main categories:

(1) National record offices and libraries financed directly by central government funds

(2) Local record offices and libraries financed by local government authorities

(3) University and college libraries and departments financed mainly from central government funds through the Universities Funding Council but in part by endowment and other income

(4) Special libraries and archives supported by privately or charitably endowed societies and institutions.

They are normally arranged in this order in the text, by county or region as appropriate.

The directory does not attempt to list the many museums and libraries which incidentally hold collections of manuscript material or the numerous other institutions and private owners who are prepared by arrangement to make their own records available for research. Their names and addresses may be found through the reference works cited on p 42. Other organisations that may be able to help students to locate papers are listed on pp 41–42.

In addition to the regular annual periods of closure noted, virtually all repositories are closed on public holidays and usually for one or more adjacent days, especially at Easter and between Christmas and New Year. Although many of the repositories listed do not require readers to make appointments, advance notice of a visit is always recommended. Readers intending to consult records commonly held on microfilm are specially advised to give advance warning of their visit. Many of the repositories listed can accommodate disabled readers with ease, but such readers are always well advised to make enquiries on this point as special arrangements may have to be made. Repositories which issue readers' tickets almost always require proof of identity before tickets can be provided.

Brief particulars of comprehensive published guides to the holdings of repositories are noted. Details of those confined to specific classes of records, typescript subject source guides and descriptions of individual collections are not noted but may be obtained from the institutions in question. Copies of the published guides and of unpublished lists of collections reported to the National Register of Archives, which is maintained by the Royal Commission on Historical Manuscripts (p 41), may be consulted in the Commission's search room.

The Commission is again grateful to repositories for providing the information in this edition. It has been edited for publication by Mary Ellis with the assistance of Peter Wojtyczka.

BS Smith
Secretary

Quality House, Quality Court, Chancery Lane, London WC2A 1HP

18 April 1991

Abbreviations

● Appointment required.

Photographs
Has in-house facilities to provide photographic copies. (Every repository listed can supply photocopies.)

Microfilm
Has in-house facilities to provide microfilm copies.

Repair
Has facilities for the repair of manuscripts
(★) can also in certain circumstances offer repair services to outside bodies or individuals on repayment.

P
Appointed by the Lord Chancellor as a repository for individually specified classes of public records under the provisions of section 4 of the Public Records Act 1958.

P(S)
Approved as a place of deposit for records held under the charge and superintendence of the Keeper of the Records of Scotland.

M&T
Recognised by the Master of the Rolls as a repository for manorial and tithe documents under the provisions of section 144A(7) of the Law of Property Act 1922, and section 36(2) of the Tithe Act 1936, as amended by section 7(1) of the Local Government (Records) Act 1962.

D
Designated by the bishop of a diocese as a repository for ecclesiastical records within that diocese. The name(s) of the diocese(s) and any qualifications are indicated in brackets.

ENGLAND

AVON

[1] **Bath City Record Office**
Guildhall, Bath BA1 5AW

Tel 0225 461111 ext 2420/1
Fax 0225 448646

City Archivist: CA Johnston

M–Th 9–1 2–5, F 9–1 2–4.30
Photographs
P

[2] **Bristol Record Office**
'B' Bond Warehouse, Smeaton
Road, Bristol BS1 6XN

Tel 0272 225692

City Archivist: JS Williams

● M–Th 9.30–4.45. Closed last
two weeks in January
Photographs Microfilm
P D (Bristol)

E Ralph, *Guide to the Bristol Archives
Office*, 1971

[3] **Bristol University Library**
Tyndall Avenue, Bristol BS8 1TJ

Tel 0272 303030 ext 8014
Fax 0272 255334

Special Collections Librarian:
NA Lee

● M–F 9–5
Letter of introduction
Photographs

BEDFORDSHIRE

[4] **Bedfordshire Record Office**
County Hall, Cauldwell Street,
Bedford MK42 9AP

Tel 0234 228833
Fax 0234 228619

County Archivist: CJ Pickford

M–F 9–1 2–5 (opens at 10 first Th
in month)
Photographs Microfilm Repair
P M&T D (St Albans: parish
records of Bedford archdeaconry)

*Guide to the Bedfordshire Record
Office*, 1957, *Guide supplement
1957–62*, nd

BERKSHIRE

[5] **Berkshire Record Office**
Shire Hall, Shinfield Park, Reading
RG2 9XD

Tel 0734 233182
Fax 0734 233203

County Archivist: P Durrant

● T–W 9–5, Th 9–9, F 9–4.30.
Closed two weeks in
October/November
Readers ticket
Photographs Microfilm Repair★
P M&T D (Oxford: Berkshire
archdeaconry)

F Hull, *Guide to the Berkshire Record
Office*, 1952

[6] **Reading University Library**
PO Box 223, Whiteknights,
Reading RG6 2AE

Tel 0734 318776

Keeper of Archives and
Manuscripts: M Bott

● T–F 9–1 2–5. Closed in August
Photographs Microfilm Repair

JA Edwards, *Brief guide to archives
and manuscripts in the library,
University of Reading*, revised edn,
1983

[7] **Institute of Agricultural History and Museum of English Rural Life**
University of Reading, PO Box 229, Whiteknights, Reading RG6 2AG

Tel 0734 318666
Fax 0734 314404

Archivist: JH Brown

● M–Th 9.30–1 2–5, F 9.30–1 2–4.30
Photographs Microfilm

Guide to the Institute of Agricultural History and Museum of English Rural Life, 1982

BUCKINGHAMSHIRE

[8] **Buckinghamshire Record Office**
County Hall, Aylesbury HP20 1UA

Tel 0296 382587
Fax 0296 383166

County Archivist: HA Hanley

● T–Th 9–5.15, F 9–4.45. Closed second week in February
Readers ticket
Photographs Repair
P M&T D (Oxford: Buckingham archdeaconry)

CAMBRIDGESHIRE

[9] **County Record Office, Cambridge**
Shire Hall, Cambridge CB3 0AP

Tel 0223 317281
Fax 0223 317201

County Archivist: JM Farrar

M–Th 9–12.45 1.45–5.15, F 9–12.45 1.45–4.15, T to 9 by appointment
Readers ticket
Repair
P M&T D (Ely: parish records of Ely archdeaconry and Ely and March deaneries)

[10] **County Record Office, Huntingdon**
Grammar School Walk, Huntingdon PE18 6LF

Tel 0480 425842
Fax 0480 425520

Deputy County Archivist: PC Saunders

M–Th 9–12.45 1.45–5.15, F 9–12.45 1.45–4.15, second S in month 9–12 by appointment
Readers ticket
Photographs Repair
P M&T D (Ely: parish records of Huntingdon archdeaconry)

GH Findlay, *Guide to the Huntingdonshire Record Office*, 1958

[11] **Cambridge University Library, Department of Manuscripts and University Archives**
West Road, Cambridge CB3 9DR

Tel 0223 333000 ext 3143 (Manuscripts), 3148 (University archives)
Fax 0223 333160

Keeper of Manuscripts and University Archives: PNR Zutshi

● M–F 9.30–6.45, S 9.30–12.30. Closed one week in September
Readers ticket
Letter of introduction
Photographs Microfilm Repair
P M&T D (Ely)

Catalogue of manuscripts preserved in the library of the University of Cambridge, 6 vols, 1856–67, reprinted 1979. AEB Owen, *Summary guide to accessions of western manuscripts (other than medieval) since 1867*, 1966. DM Owen, *Cambridge University Archives: a classified list*, 1989

Royal Greenwich Observatory Archives

Tel 0223 333142
Fax 0223 333160

Archivist: AJ Perkins

● M–F 9.30–6.45, S 9.30–12.30. Closed one week in September
Readers ticket

[12] **Centre of South Asian Studies**
Laundress Lane, Cambridge
CB2 1SD

Tel 0223 338094

Secretary/Librarian: LJ Carter

● M–F 9.30–5. Closed in August
Letter of introduction
Photographs Microfilm

Principal collections of papers in the Cambridge South Asian Archive, 2nd edn, 1987

[13] **Churchill Archives Centre**
Churchill College, Cambridge
CB3 0DS

Tel 0223 336087
Fax 0223 336177

Keeper: CD Barnett

● M–F 9–12.30 1.30–5
Letter of introduction
Repair

A guide to the holdings of the Churchill Archives Centre, 1988

[14] **King's College Library, Modern Archive Centre**
King's College, Cambridge
CB2 1ST

Tel 0223 350411 ext 423

Modern Archivist: Ms J Cox

● M–F 9.30–12.30 1.30–5.15
Letter of introduction
Repair

[15] **Scott Polar Research Institute**
Lensfield Road, Cambridge
CB2 1ER

Tel 0223 336555
Fax 0223 336549

Archivist: RK Headland

● M–F 10–12.30 2.30–5
Repair
P

C Holland, *Manuscripts in the Scott Polar Research Institute*, 1982

[16] **Trinity College Library**
Trinity College, Cambridge
CB1 1TQ

Tel 0223 338488
Fax 0223 338564

Archivist: AM Kucia

● M–F 9–5
Letter of introduction
Photographs

MR James, *The western manuscripts in the library of Trinity College, Cambridge*, 3 vols, 1900–2

CHESHIRE

[17] **Cheshire Record Office**
Duke Street, Chester CH1 1RL

Tel 0244 602559

Principal Archivist: J Pepler

● M–F 9.15–4.45 (second W in month to 8.30), fourth S in month 10–1
Repair
P M&T D (Chester. Liverpool: parish records of Warrington and Farnworth deaneries)

CM Williams, *Guide to the Cheshire Record Office*, 1991

[18] **Chester City Record Office**
Town Hall, Chester CH1 2HJ

Tel 0244 324324 ext 2108
Fax 0244 324338

City Archivist: Mrs M Lewis

M 9.30–7.30, T–Th 9.30–5.30, F 9.30–5
Photographs Repair
P M&T

AM Kennett, *Archives and records of the City of Chester*, 1985

[19] **Warrington Library**
Museum Street, Warrington
WA1 1JB

Tel 0925 571232
Fax 0925 411395

Area Librarian: D Rogers

● M–W, F 9–7, Th 9.30–1, S 9–1
M&T

CLEVELAND

[20] **Cleveland Archives Section**
Exchange House, 6 Marton Road,
Middlesbrough TS1 1DB

Tel 0642 248321

County Archivist: DH Tyrell

● M–Th 9–1 2–4.30, F 9–1 2–4
Readers ticket
Photographs Repair
P D (York: Cleveland parish
records)

CORNWALL

[21] **Cornwall Record Office**
County Hall, Truro TR1 3AY

Tel 0872 73698/74282
Fax 0872 222490

County Archivist: Mrs CR North

● T–Th 9.30–1 2–5, F 9.30–1
2–4.30, S 9–12. Closed first two
weeks in December
Readers ticket
Photographs Microfilm Repair
P M&T D (Truro)

Brief guide to sources, 2nd edn, 1985

[22] **Royal Institution of
Cornwall**
Royal Cornwall Museum, River
Street, Truro TR1 2SJ

Tel 0872 72205

Librarian: Ms A Broome

Address correspondence to the
Courtney Library at the above
address
M–S 10–1 2–5

CUMBRIA

[23] **Cumbria Record Office,
Carlisle**
The Castle, Carlisle CA3 8UR

Tel 0228 23456 ext 2416

County Archivist:
Miss SJ MacPherson
Assistant County Archivist:
DM Bowcock

M–F 9–5
Readers ticket
Photographs Microfilm Repair
P M&T D (Carlisle)

[24] **Cumbria Record Office,
Kendal**
County Offices, Kendal LA9 4RQ

Tel 0539 721000 ext 4329

County Archivist:
Miss SJ MacPherson
Assistant County Archivist:
JM Grisenthwaite

M–F 9–5
Readers ticket
P M&T D (Carlisle. Bradford:
parish records)

[25] **Cumbria Record Office,
Barrow**
140 Duke Street, Barrow-in-
Furness LA14 1XW

Tel 0229 831269

Area Archivist: ACJ Jones

M–F 9–5
Readers ticket
P M&T D (Carlisle: Furness
archdeaconry)
P

DERBYSHIRE

[26] **Derbyshire Record Office**
New Street, Matlock

Tel 0629 580000 ext 7347
Fax 0629 580350

County Archivist:
Margaret O'Sullivan

Address correspondence to
Education Department, County
Offices, Matlock DE4 3AG

● M–F 9.30–1 2–4.45
Repair★
P M&T D (Derby)

DEVON

[27] **Devon Record Office**
Castle Street, Exeter EX4 3PU

Tel 0392 384253
Fax 0392 272798

County Archivist: Mrs MM Rowe

M–Th 9.30–5, F 9.30–4.30, first
and third S in month 9.30–12
Admission fee
Photographs Microfilm Repair★
P M&T D (Exeter)

[28] **North Devon Record
Office**
North Devon Library and Record
Office, Tuly Street, Barnstaple
EX32 7EJ

Tel 0271 47119
Fax 0271 47172

Senior Assistant Archivist:
Ms LMA Rose

M, T, F 9.30–5, W 9.30–4,
Th 9.30–7, two S in month 9.30–4
Admission fee
P M&T D (Exeter: Barnstaple
archdeaconry)

[29] **West Devon Area Record
Office**
Unit 3, Clare Place, Coxside,
Plymouth PL4 0JW

Tel 0752 385940

Senior Assistant Archivist:
P Brough

M–Th 9.30–5, to 7 first W in
month, F 9.30–4.30
Admission fee
P M&T D (Exeter: Plymouth
archdeaconry)

[30] **Exeter University Library**
Stocker Road, Exeter EX4 4PT

Tel 0392 263870

University Librarian: JF Stirling

● M–F 9–5.30
Readers ticket
Photographs Microfilm

Manuscript collections, 1976

DORSET

[31] **Dorset Record Office**
Bridport Road, Dorchester
DT1 1RP

Tel 0305 250550
Fax 0305 204839

County Archivist: H Jaques

● M–F 9–5, S 9.30–12.30
Photographs Microfilm Repair★
P M&T D (Salisbury: parish
records of Dorset and Sherborne
archdeaconries)

DURHAM

[32] **Durham County Record
Office**
County Hall, Durham DH1 5UL

Tel 091–386 4411 ext 2575

County Archivist: Miss J Gill

● M, T, Th 8.45–4.45,
W 8.45–8.30, F 8.45–4.15
Photographs Microfilm Repair
P M&T D (Durham. Ripon: parish
records)

WAL Seaman, *Durham County
Record Office*, 1969

[33] **Durham County Record
Office, Darlington Library**
Local History Section
Crown Street, Darlington
DL1 1ND

Tel 0325 469858

Branch Archivist: Post vacant

M–F 9–1 2–7, S 9–1 2–5

[34] **Durham University Library, Archives and Special Collections**
Palace Green Section, Palace Green, Durham DH1 3RN

Tel 091–374 3001
Fax 091–374 3741

Sub-Librarian (Special Collections): Miss EM Rainey

Term: M–F 9–6, S 9–12.30
Vacation: M–F 9–5
Photographs Microfilm Repair
M&T

D Ramage, *Summary list of additional manuscripts accessioned and listed between September 1945 and September 1961*, 1963

5 The College,
Durham DH1 3EQ

Tel 091–374 3610
Fax 091–374 3741

Senior Assistant Keeper: JM Fewster

M–F 9–1 2–5, T 5–8 during term by arrangement. Closed for three weeks in summer
Photographs Microfilm Repair
P M&T D (Durham)

The Prior's Kitchen,
The College, Durham DH1 3EQ

Tel 091–374 3615
Fax 091–374 3741

Senior Assistant Keeper: P Mussett

M–F 9–1 2–5, T 5–8 during term by arrangement. Closed for three weeks in summer
Photographs Microfilm Repair
P M&T D (Durham)

ESSEX

[35] **Essex Record Office**
PO Box 11, County Hall,
Chelmsford CM1 1LX

Tel 0245 492211 430 067
Fax 0245 352710

County Archivist: VW Gray

● M 10–8.45, T–Th 9.15–5.15, F 9.15–4.15
Readers ticket
Photographs Microfilm Repair★
P M&T D (Chelmsford)

FG Emmison, *Guide to the Essex Record Office*, 1969

[36] **Essex Record Office, Colchester and North-East Essex Branch**
Stanwell House, Stanwell Street, Colchester CO2 7DL

Tel 0206 572099

Branch Archivist: PRJ Coverley

● M 10–5.15 (8.45 on second M in month), T–Th 9.15–5.15, F 9.15–4.15
Readers ticket
P M&T D (Chelmsford: NE Essex parish records)

[37] **Essex Record Office, Southend Branch**
Central Library, Victoria Avenue, Southend-on-Sea SS2 6EX

Tel 0702 612621

Branch Archivist: JR Smith

● M, W, Th 9.15–5.15, T 9.45–5.15, F 9.15–4.15
Readers ticket
Photographs Repair★
M&T D (Chelmsford: SE Essex parish records)

GLOUCESTERSHIRE

[38] **Gloucestershire Record Office**
Clarence Row, Alvin Street, Gloucester GL1 3DW

Tel 0452 425295

County Archivist: DJH Smith

M–W, F 9–5, Th 9–8
Readers ticket. Admission fee
Photographs Microfilm Repair
P M&T D (Gloucester)

Handlist of the contents of the Gloucestershire Record Office, 2nd edn, 1990

HAMPSHIRE

[39] Hampshire Record Office
20 Southgate Street, Winchester
SO23 9EF

Tel 0962 846142/846154
Fax 0962 867273

County Archivist:
Miss RC Dunhill

M–Th 9–4.45, F 9–4.15, S 9–12.
Closed last full week before
Christmas
Readers ticket
Photographs Microfilm Repair
P M&T D (Winchester, except
Southampton. Portsmouth: parish
records of Petersfield and Bishops
Waltham deaneries)

[40] Portsmouth City Records Office
3 Museum Road, Portsmouth
PO1 2LE

Tel 0705 829765
Fax 0705 828441

City Records Officer:
Mrs SE Quail

M–Th 9.30–5, F 9.30–4, closed to
1.15 first M of month
Readers ticket
Photographs Microfilm Repair★
P M&T D (Portsmouth: parish
records of Portsmouth, Havant,
Fareham and Gosport deaneries)

[41] Southampton City Records Office
Civic Centre, Southampton SO9
4XR

Tel 0703 832251/223855 ext 2251
Fax 0703 832424

Archives and Records Manager:
Mrs SL Woolgar

M–F 9–5, one evening a month to
9
Photographs Repair
P M&T D (Winchester:
Southampton parish records)

[42] Southampton University Library
Highfield, Southampton SO9 5NH

Tel 0703 593724/592721
Fax 0703 593939

Archivist: CM Woolgar

● Term: M, T, F 9–5, W 10–5,
Th 9–7, Vacation: M–F 9–5
Photographs Microfilm Repair

HEREFORD AND WORCESTER

[43] Hereford and Worcester Record Office
County Hall, Spetchley Road,
Worcester WR5 2NP

Tel 0905 763763 ext 6350
Fax 0905 763000

County Archivist: AM Wherry

● M 10–4.45, T–Th 9.15–4.45,
F 9.15–4
Readers ticket
Photographs Microfilm Repair★
P D (Worcester)

[44] Hereford Record Office
The Old Barracks, Harold Street,
Hereford HR1 2QX

Tel 0432 265441

Assistant Head of Record Services:
Miss DS Hubbard

M 10–1 2–4.45, T–Th 9.15–1
2–4.45, F 9.15–1 2–4
Readers ticket
Microfilm Repair★
P M&T D (Hereford)

[45] Worcester (St Helen's) Record Office
Fish Street, Worcester WR1 2HN

Tel 0905 763763 ext 5922

Assistant County Archivist:
R Whittaker

M 10–4.45, T–Th 9.15–4.45,
F 9.15–4
Readers ticket
P M&T D (Worcester)

HERTFORDSHIRE

[46] Hertfordshire Record Office
County Hall, Hertford SG13 8DE

Tel 0992 555105
Fax 0992 555644

County Archivist:
Kathryn M Thompson

M–Th 9.15–5.15, F 9.15–4.30
Readers ticket
Photographs Repair
P M&T D (St Albans)

HUMBERSIDE

[47] Humberside County Archive Office
County Hall, Beverley HU17 9BA

Tel 0482 885005/7
Fax 0482 885035

County Archivist: KD Holt

● M, W, Th 9.15–4.45, T 9.15–8,
F 9.15–4. Closed last week in
January
Microfilm Repair*
P M&T D (York: parish records of
the East Riding archdeaconry)

[48] South Humberside Area Archive Office
Town Hall Square, Grimsby
DN31 1HX

Tel 0472 353481

Archivist in charge: JF Wilson

● M–Th 9.30–12 1–5, F 9.30–12
1–4.15
Repair
P M&T

*South Humberside Area Record Office:
summary guide, 1989*

[49] Kingston upon Hull City Record Office
79 Lowgate, Kingston upon Hull
HU1 2AA

Tel 0482 595102/595110
Fax 0482 213170

Archivist: GW Oxley

● M–Th 8.30–4.45, F 8.30–4.15
W 5–8 by arrangement
Photographs Microfilm Repair
P M&T

[50] Hull University, Brynmor Jones Library
Cottingham Road, Hull HU6 7RX

Tel 0482 465265
Fax 0482 466205

Archivist: B Dyson

● M–F 9–1 2–5
Photographs Microfilm
M&T

KENT

[51] Centre for Kentish Studies
County Hall, Maidstone
ME14 1XQ

Tel 0622 694363

Acting Head of Heritage Services:
Miss KM Topping

● T–F 9–5, second and fourth S in
month 9–1. Closed two weeks in
spring and autumn
Readers ticket. Admission fee
(overseas researchers)
Photographs Microfilm
P M&T D (Rochester: Rochester
and Tonbridge archdeaconries
excluding Gillingham, Rochester
and Strood rural deaneries.
Canterbury: Maidstone
archdeaconry)

F Hull, *Guide to the Kent County
Archives Office*, 1958, *First
supplement*, 1971, *Second supplement*,
1983

[52] **Canterbury City and Cathedral Archives**
The Precincts, Canterbury
CT1 2EG

Tel 0227 463510

Cathedral Archivist:
Mrs CA Hodgson

● M–Th 9–5. Closed two weeks
in spring and autumn
Readers ticket. Admission fee
(overseas researchers)
Photographs Microfilm Repair★
P M&T D (Canterbury:
Canterbury archdeaconry)

[53] **Shepway Branch Archives Office**
Central Library, Grace Hill,
Folkestone CT20 1HD

Tel 0303 850123

Group Manager: D Paynter

● M, Th 9–6, T, F 9–7, W 9–1,
S 9–5
Photographs Microfilm

[54] **Thanet Branch Archives Office**
Ramsgate Library, Guildford
Lawn, Ramsgate CT11 9AI

Tel 0843 593532

Group Manager: Mrs H Halse

● M–W 9.30–6, Th, S 9.30–5,
F 9.30–8
Photographs Microfilm

[55] **Medway Area Archives Office**
Civic Centre, Strood, Rochester
ME2 4AW

Tel 0634 732714
Fax 0634 732756

Area Archivist: SM Dixon

● M–Th 9–12.45 2–4.45, F
9–12.45
Readers ticket
Photographs Microfilm
P M&T D (Rochester: Gillingham,
Rochester and Strood rural
deaneries)

[56] **Sevenoaks Branch Archives Office**
Central Library, Buckhurst Lane,
Sevenoaks TN13 1LQ

Tel 0732 452384

Group Manager: Mrs L Rich

● M–W, F 9.30–5.30, Th 9.30–7,
S 9–5
Photographs Microfilm

LANCASHIRE

[57] **Lancashire Record Office**
Bow Lane, Preston PR1 2RE

Tel 0772 54868 ext 3039/3041

County Archivist: K Hall

T 9–8.30, W–F 9–5
Readers ticket
Microfilm Repair
P M&T D (Blackburn, Bradford:
parish records. Liverpool: northern
deaneries. Richmond
archdeaconry)

RS France, *Guide to the Lancashire
Record Office,* 3rd edn, 1985

LEICESTERSHIRE

[58] **Leicestershire Record Office**
57 New Walk, Leicester LE1 7JB

Tel 0533 544566
Fax 0533 317820

County Archivist: CW Harrison

M–Th 9.15–5, F 9.15–4.45, S
9.15–12.15. Closed first week in
October
Readers ticket
Photographs Microfilm Repair★
P M&T D (Leicester.
Peterborough: Rutland parish
records)

LINCOLNSHIRE

[59] Lincolnshire Archives
St Rumbold Street, Lincoln
LN2 5AB

Tel 0522 525158/526204

Principal Archivist: GA Knight

● M 2–7.45, T–F 9–5, S 9–4
Readers ticket. Admission fee
Photographs Microfilm Repair★
P D (Lincoln)

GREATER LONDON: NATIONAL REPOSITORIES

[60] British Library, Manuscript Collections
Great Russell Street, London
WC1B 3DG

Tel 071–323 7513 ext 4
Fax 071–323 7745

Director of Special Collections:
Alice MS Prochaska

M–S 10–4.45. Closed one week in
November
Readers ticket. Letter of
introduction
Photographs Microfilm Repair★
P M&T

MAE Nickson, *The British Library: guide to the catalogues and indexes of the Department of Manuscripts*, 1978. *Catalogue of additions 1946–50*, 3 vols, 1979. *Catalogue of additions 1951–55*, 3 vols, 1982. *Index of MSS in the British Library*, 10 vols, 1984–86.

[61] British Library, Oriental and India Office Collections
197 Blackfriars Road, London
SE1 8NG

Tel 071–412 7000/7873
Fax 071–412 7641/7858

Director of Special Collections:
Alice MS Prochaska
Deputy Director (India Office Collections): AJ Farrington ·

M–F 9.30–5.45, S 9.30–12.45
Readers ticket
Photographs Microfilm Repair
P

M Moir, *A general guide to the India Office Records*, 1988

[62] House of Lords Record Office
House of Lords, London
SW1A 0PW

Tel 071–219 3074
Fax 071–219 6715

Clerk of the Records: DJ Johnson

● M–F 9.30–5. Closed last two
weeks in November
Photographs Microfilm Repair

MF Bond, *Guide to the records of Parliament*, 1971

[63] Imperial War Museum, Department of Documents
Lambeth Road, London SE1 6HZ

Tel 071–416 5221/2
Fax 071–416 5374

Keeper of the Department of
Documents: RWA Suddaby

● M–S 10–5. Closed last two full
weeks in November
Photographs Microfilm
P

[64] National Army Museum, Department of Archives, Photographs, Film and Sound
Royal Hospital Road, Chelsea,
London SW3 4HT

Tel 071–730 0717 ext 212
Fax 071–823 6573

Head of Department of Archives:
PB Boyden

T–S 10–4.30. Closed last two full
weeks in October
Readers ticket
Photographs Microfilm Repair
P

[65] **National Maritime Museum, Manuscripts Section**
Greenwich, London SE10 9NF

Tel 081–858 4422 ext 6722
Fax 081–312 6632

Head of Manuscripts Section:
Ms C MacLeod

M–F 10–5, S 10–1 2–5 by appointment only. Closed one week in February
Readers ticket
Photographs Microfilm Repair
P

RJB Knight, *Guide to the manuscripts in the National Maritime Museum*, 2 vols, 1977, 1980

[66] **The Natural History Museum**
Cromwell Road, London SW7 5BD

Tel 071–938 9238/8972
Fax 071–938 9290

Museum Archivist: JC Thackray

● M–F 10–4
Readers ticket
Photographs
P

Catalogue of the books, manuscripts, maps and drawings in the British Museum (Natural History), 5 vols and 3 supplementary vols, 1903–40. FC Sawyer, *A short history of the libraries and list of manuscripts and original drawings in the British Museum (Natural History)*, 1971

[67] **Public Record Office**
Ruskin Avenue, Kew, Richmond TW9 4DU

Tel 081–876 3444
Fax 081–878 8905 ext 2497

Chancery Lane, London ✳
WC2A 1LR

Tel 081–876 3444
Fax 081–878 7231 ext 2216

Keeper of Public Records:
Mrs SJ Tyacke

M–F 9.30–5. Closed first two weeks in October
Readers ticket
Photographs Microfilm Repair★

Guide to the contents of the Public Record Office, 3 vols, 1963, 1968

The records now remaining at Chancery Lane comprise all those described in Vol 1 of the *Guide* (except the Copyright Office), those of some other departments, etc with quasi-legal or related functions, the records of the State Paper Office, the Probate records and some gifts and deposits.

[68] **Royal Air Force Museum, Department of Aviation Records**
Grahame Park Way, Hendon, London NW9 5LL

Tel 081–205 2266 ext 210/211/250
Fax 081–200 1751

Keeper of Aviation Records:
PG Murton

● M–F 10–5.30
Photographs Microfilm
P

[69] **Royal Botanic Gardens, Kew, Library and Archives**
Kew, Richmond TW9 3AE

Tel 081–332 5411/5417
Fax 081–332 5278

Chief Librarian and Archivist:
Miss SMD FitzGerald

● M–Th 9–5.30, F 9–5
Readers ticket
Photographs Repair
P

[70] **Science Museum Library**
South Kensington, London
SW7 5NH

Tel 071–938 8234/8218
Fax 071–938 8213

Archivist: RW Sharp

● M–S 10–5.30
Readers ticket
Photographs Microfilm
P

[71] **Tate Gallery Archive**
Millbank, London SW1P 4RG

Tel 071–821 1313 ext 201/322
Fax 071–931 7687

Head of Archive and Registry:
Mrs J Booth

● Th, F 10–1 2–5.30
Letter of introduction
Photographs Repair
P

Tate Gallery Archive: an index on microfiche, 1986

[72] **Victoria & Albert Museum, National Art Library**
Cromwell Road, London
SW7 2RL

Tel 071–938 8314/5
Fax 071–938 8461

Head of Special Collections:
R Watson

T–S 10–5. Closed first two weeks in September
Readers ticket. Letter of introduction
Photographs Microfilm Repair

[73] **Victoria & Albert Museum, Archive of Art and Design**
23 Blythe Road, London W14 0QF

Tel 071–603 1514
Fax 071–602 6907

Curator in charge: Ms MM Sweet

● T–Th 10–1 2–4.30. Closed first two weeks in September
Letter of introduction
Photographs Repair

GREATER LONDON:
LOCAL REPOSITORIES

[74] **Greater London Record Office and History Library**
40 Northampton Road, London
EC1R 0HB

Tel 071–606 3030 ext 3820
Fax 071–833 9136

Head Archivist: Miss J Coburn

T–F 9.30–4.45, T to 7.30 by appointment. Closed third and fourth weeks in October
Repair
P M&T D (London. Southwark. Guildford)

[75] **Corporation of London Records Office**
PO Box 270, Guildhall, London
EC2P 2EJ

Tel 071–260 1251/071–606 3030 ext 1251
Fax 071–260 1119

City Archivist: JR Sewell

M–F 9.30–4.45
Microfilm Repair
P M&T

PE Jones and R Smith, *Guide to the records at Guildhall, London, part 1 the Corporation of London Records Office*, 1951

[76] **Guildhall Library**
Aldermanbury, London EC2P 2EJ

Tel 071–260 1862/3
Fax 071–260 1119

Keeper of Manuscripts:
SGH Freeth

M–S 9.30–4.45
Photographs Microfilm Repair
P M&T D (London)

J Bullock-Anderson, C Clubb and
J Cox, *Guide to archives and
manuscripts at Guildhall Library*, 1989

[77] **Barnet Archives and Local
Studies Centre**
Hendon Catholic Social Centre,
Chapel Walk, Egerton Gardens,
London NW4 4BE

Tel 081–202 5625 ext 55
Fax 081–202 8520

Borough Archivists:
Mrs JM Corden, Ms PJ Taylor

Address correspondence to
Ravensfield House, The
Burroughs, Hendon, London
NW4 4BE

● M–W, F 9.30–5, Th 9.30–7.30,
S 9.30–4
Photographs
M&T

Guide to archives and records (revised
edition in preparation)

[78] **Bexley Libraries and
Museums Department**
Local Studies Centre, Hall Place,
Bourne Road, Bexley DA5 1PQ

Tel 0322 526574 ext 217/8
Fax 0322 522921

Local Studies Officer/Archivist:
MD Barr-Hamilton

M–S 9–5 (in winter 9 to dusk)
D (Rochester: parish records of
Erith and Sidcup deaneries)

[79] **Bromley Public Libraries,
Archives Section**
Central Library, High Street,
Bromley BR1 1EX

Tel 081–460 9955 ext 261/2
Fax 081–313 0475

Archivist: Miss E Silverthorne

● M, W, F, 9.30–6,
T, Th 9.30–8, S 9.30–5
Photographs Microfilm
P D (Rochester: parish records of
Beckenham, Bromley and
Orpington deaneries)

[80] **Camden Leisure Services,
Swiss Cottage Library**
Local Studies Library,
88 Avenue Road,
London NW3 3HA

Tel 071–413 6522

Local Studies Librarian/Archivist:
MJ Holmes

M, Th 10–7, T 10–6, S 10–5
Photographs Microfilm Repair

*The Local Studies Library: a guide to
the collections*, 1990

Camden Leisure Services,
Holborn Library
Local Studies Library,
32–38 Theobalds Road,
London WC1X 8PA

Tel 071–413 6342

Assistant Local Studies
Librarian/Archivist: RG Knight

● M 10–1 2–7, T, F 10–1 2–6, S
by arrangement
Photographs Microfilm Repair

[81] **Greenwich Local History Library**
Woodlands, 90 Mycenae Road,
Blackheath, London SE3 7SE

Tel 081–858 4631

Local History Librarian: J Watson

● M, T 9–5.30, Th 9–8, S 9–5
Photographs
P D (Southwark: Charlton,
Kidbrooke, St George's
Westcombe Park parish records)

[82] **Hackney Archives Department**
Rose Lipman Library, De Beauvoir
Road, London N1 5SQ

Tel: 071–241 2886

Archivist: DL Mander

● M, T, Th, first and third S in
month 9.30–1 2–5
Photographs Microfilm Repair*
P

[83] **Hammersmith and Fulham Archives**
The Lilla Huset,
191 Talgarth Road,
London W6 8BJ

Tel 081–741 5159
Fax 081–741 4882

Borough Archivist: JJ Farrell

● M 9.30–8, T, Th, first S in
month 9.30–1
Photographs Repair

[84] **Haringey Community Information**
Bruce Castle Museum, Lordship
Lane, London N17 8NU

Tel 081–808 8772

Archivist: Ms J Kimber

By appointment only
Photographs Microfilm
M&T

[85] **Kensington and Chelsea Libraries and Arts Service**
Central Library, Phillimore Walk,
London W8 7RX
Public entrance is in Hornton
Street

Tel 071–937 2542 ext 3004/3038
Fax 071–937 0515

Local Studies Librarian:
Mrs C Starren

● M 10–1 2–8, Th 10–8, F, S 10–1
2–5
Photographs

*A short guide to the Kensington and
Chelsea local collections, 1983*

[86] **Lambeth Archives Department**
Minet Library, 52 Knatchbull
Road, London SE5 9QY

Tel 071–926 6076

Borough Archivist: JA Newman

● M 10.30–7.30, T, Th, alternate
S 9.30–1 2–4.30
Photographs Microfilm
M&T

[87] **Lewisham Local History Centre**
The Manor House, Old Road, Lee,
London SE13 5SY

Tel 081–852 5050/7087
Fax 081–297 0927

Archivist: Jean Wait

M, Th 9.30–1 2–5, T 9.30–1 2–8
Photographs
P M&T D (Southwark: parish
records of East and West
Lewisham deaneries)

[88] **Redbridge Central Library**
Local History Room, Clements
Road, Ilford IG1 1EA

Tel 081–478 7145
Fax 081–553 4185

Local History Librarian: I Dowling

T–F 9.30–8, S 9.30–4
Photographs Microfilm

[89] Southwark Local Studies Library
211 Borough High Street, London
SE1 1JA

Tel 071–403 3507

Local Studies Librarian:
Nicola Smith
Assistant Local Studies Librarian
and Archivist: SC Humphrey

● M, Th 9.30–12.30 1.30–8,
T, F 9.30–12.30 1.30–5, S 9–1

[90] Tower Hamlets Libraries Local History Library and Archives
Central Library, 277 Bancroft
Road, London E1 4DQ

Tel 081–980 4366

Archivist: CJ Lloyd

M, Th 9–8, T, F 9–6, W, S 9–5
Photographs Microfilm

[91] Waltham Forest Archives
Vestry House Museum, Vestry
Road, Walthamstow, London
E17 9NH

Tel 081–509 1917/081–527 5544
ext 4391

Local Studies and Museums
Officer: RJ Colori

By arrangement only
Photographs
M&T D (Chelmsford: parish
records of Waltham Forest
deanery)

[92] Westminster City Archives
Victoria Library, 160 Buckingham
Palace Road, London SW1W 9UD

Tel 071–798 2180
Fax 071–798 2181

Chief Archivist:
Miss MJ Swarbrick

M–F 9.30–7, S 9.30–1 2–5
Photographs Microfilm Repair
P M&T D (London: Westminster
parish records)

Marylebone Library
Marylebone Road, London
NW1 5PS

Tel 071–798 1030
Fax 071–798 1019

Archivist: RA Bowden

● M 10–7, T, W, F 9.30–5,
Th 9.30–7, S 9.30–1 2–5
Photographs Microfilm
P M&T

GREATER LONDON:
UNIVERSITY REPOSITORIES

[93] University of London Library
Palaeography Room, Senate
House, Malet Street, London
WC1E 7HU

Tel 071–636 4514 ext 5030

Archivist: Ms B Weeden

● M–F 10–5. Closed one week in
July
Readers ticket
Photographs Microfilm Repair★
M&T

RA Rye, *Catalogue of the manuscripts
and autograph letters in the University
Library . . .*, 1921, *Supplement
1921–30*, 1930. *Catalogue of the
Goldsmiths Library of Economic
Literature*, vols iii and iv, 1982,
1983. J Percival, *A guide to archives
and manuscripts in the University of
London*, vol 1, 1984

[94] British Library of Political and Economic Science
10 Portugal Street, London
WC2A 2HD

Tel 071–955 7223
Fax 071–242 0392

Archivist: GEA Raspin

Term: M–F 10–5.30, Vacation:
10–5. Closed for one week at
Easter, Christmas and in the
summer
Readers ticket
Photographs Microfilm

J Percival, *op cit*

[95] Imperial College Archives
Room 455, Sherfield Building,
Imperial College, London
SW7 2AZ

Tel 071–589 5111 ext 3022
Fax 071–584 7596

College Archivist: Mrs A Barrett

● M–F 10–12.30 2–5
Letter of introduction
Photographs

A guide to Imperial College Archives,
1982. J Percival, *op cit*

**[96] Institute of
Commonwealth Studies**
27–28 Russell Square, London
WC1B 5DS

Tel 071–580 5876
Fax 071–255 2160

Senior Assistant Librarian: D Blake

● Term: M–W 10–7, Th–F 10–6,
Vacation: M–F 10–5.30
Letter of introduction

**[97] King's College London,
Liddell Hart Centre for Military
Archives**
The Library, Strand, London
WC2R 2LS

Tel 071–873 2187/2015

College Archivist: Miss
PJ Methven

● Term: M–F 9.30–5.30,
Vacation: 9.30–4.30. Closed last
two weeks in August
Letter of introduction
Photographs Microfilm
P

*King's College London, manuscripts
and private papers: a select guide*,
1982. *Liddell Hart Centre for Military
Archives, consolidated list of accessions*,
1986, *Supplement August 1985–
March 1988*, 1988. J Percival, *op cit*

**[98] School of Oriental and
African Studies Library**
Thornhaugh Street, Russell
Square, London WC1H 0XG

Tel 071–323 6112
Fax 071–436 3844

Archivist: Mrs RE Seton

● M–Th 9–8.45, F 9–7, S 9.30–5,
Summer Vacation: M–F 9–5,
S 9.30–5
Readers ticket. Letter of
introduction
Photographs Microfilm

*Guide to the archives and manuscript
collections*, 1987. J Percival, *op cit*

**[99] University College
London, Manuscripts Room**
The Library, Gower Street,
London WC1E 6BT

Tel 071–387 7050 ext 2617/8
Fax 071–380 7373

Archivist: Ms GM Furlong

● Term: M, W–F 10–5,
T 10–7, Vacation: M–F 10–5
Readers ticket. Letter of
introduction preferred
Admission fee (only in special
circumstances)
Photographs Microfilm

DK Coveney, *Descriptive catalogue
of manuscripts in the library of
University College London*, 1935.
J Percival, *op cit*

GREATER LONDON:
SPECIAL REPOSITORIES

**[100] British Architectural
Library**
Royal Institute of British
Architects, Manuscripts and
Archives Collection, 66 Portland
Place, London W1N 4AD

Tel 071–580 5533 ext 4321
Fax 071–631 1802

Archivist: Mrs A Mace

M 10–5, T–Th 10–8, F 10–7,
S 10–1.30. Closed in August
Photographs Repair

A Mace, *The Royal Institute of British Architects: a guide to its archive and history*, 1986

Drawings Collection, 21 Portman Square, London W1H 9HP

Tel 071–580 5533 ext 4801

Curator of Drawings: Mrs J Lever

● M–F 10–1. Closed in August

J Lever, *Catalogue of the drawings collection. . .*, 21 vols, 1968–81

[101] **Fawcett Library**
City of London Polytechnic, Old Castle Street, London E1 7NT

Tel 071–247 5826

Reference Librarian: D Doughan

Term: M 11–8.30, W–F 10–5, Vacation: M, W–F 10–5
Admission fee

[102] **Institution of Civil Engineers**
1–7 Great George Street, London SW1P 3AA

Tel 071–222 7722 ext 232/205
Fax 071–222 7500

Archivist: Mrs MK Murphy

● M–F 9.15–5.30
Letter of introduction
Photographs

[103] **Institution of Electrical Engineers**
Archives Department, Savoy Place, London WC2R 0BL

Tel 071–240 1871 ext 336/290
Fax 071–240 7735

Archivist: Mrs EDP Symons

● M–F 10–5

[104] **Lambeth Palace Library**
London SE1 7JU

Tel 071–928 6222

Librarian: RJ Palmer

M–F 10–5. Closed ten days from Christmas Eve and ten days from Good Friday
Letter of introduction
Photographs Microfilm Repair
P M&T

HJ Todd, *Catalogue of the archiepiscopal manuscripts . . .*, 1812, continued by EGW Bill, *Catalogue of manuscripts . . .*, 3 vols, 1972–83

[105] **Linnean Society of London**
Burlington House, Piccadilly, London W1V 0LQ

Tel 071–434 4479/4470
Fax 071–287 9364

Librarian and Archivist: Miss G Douglas

● M–F 10–5

Catalogue of the manuscripts in the library of the Linnean Society of London, parts 1–4, 1934–48

[106] **Religious Society of Friends (Quakers) Library**
Friends House, Euston Road, London NW1 2BJ

Tel 071–387 3601
Fax 071–388 1977

Librarian: MJ Thomas

T–F 10–5. Closed one week before Spring Bank Holiday and one week at the end of November
Letter of introduction
Photographs

[107] **Royal College of Physicians of London**
11 St Andrews Place, Regents Park, London NW1 4LE

Tel 071–935 1174
Fax 071–487 5218

Librarian: G Davenport

M–F 9.30–5.30
P

[108] **Royal College of Surgeons of England**
35–43 Lincoln's Inn Fields, London WC2A 3PN

Tel 071–405 3474 ext 3000
Fax 071–831 9438

Librarian: IF Lyle

● M–F 10–6. Closed in August
Photographs
P

[109] **Royal Commonwealth Society Library**
18 Northumberland Avenue, London WC2N 5BJ

Tel 071–930 6733
Fax 071–930 9705

Librarian: Miss TA Barringer

● M–F 9.30–12.30 1.30–5.30
Readers ticket

DH Simpson, *The manuscript catalogue of the library . . .*, 1975

[110] **Royal Institution of Great Britain**
21 Albemarle Street, London W1X 4BS

Tel 071–409 2992 ext 4

Librarian/Archivist: Mrs IM McCabe

● M–F 10–5.30
Photographs Microfilm
P

[111] **Royal Society**
6 Carlton House Terrace, London SW1Y 5AG

Tel 071–839 5561 ext 304/261
Fax 071–930 2170

Librarian: Mrs SM Edwards
Archivist: Ms M Sampson

● M–F 10–5
Microfilm Repair

RK Bluhm, 'A guide to the archives of the Royal Society and to other manuscripts in its possession', *Notes and records of the Royal Society of London XII*, 1956–57

[112] **Society of Antiquaries of London**
Burlington House, Piccadilly, London W1V 0HS

Tel 071–734 0193/071–437 9954
Fax 071–287 6967

Librarian: EB Nurse

● M–F 10–5. Closed in August
Letter of introduction

[113] **Wellcome Institute for the History of Medicine**
Bentley House, 200 Euston Road, London NW1 2BQ

Address correspondence to 183 Euston Road, London NW1 2BN

Tel 071–383 4414
Fax 071–388 3164

Curator of Western Manuscripts: RK Aspin

M, W, F 9.45–5.15,
T, Th 9.45–7.30
Readers ticket
Photographs Microfilm Repair

SAJ Moorat, *Catalogue of western manuscripts on medicine and science in the Wellcome Historical Medical Library*, 3 vols, 1962, 1973.
WR Dawson, *Manuscripta medica, a descriptive catalogue of the manuscripts in the Library of the Medical Society of London*, 1932

Contemporary Medical Archives
Centre

Tel 071–383 4414
Fax 071–388 3164

Archivist: Miss JGA Sheppard

M, W, F 9.45–5.15,
T, Th 9.45–7.30
Readers ticket
Photographs Microfilm Repair

J Sheppard and L Hall, *A guide to
the Contemporary Medical Archives
Centre*, 1991

The Wellcome Institute for the
History of Medicine and the
Contemporary Medical Archives
Centre will move back to 183
Euston Road late in 1992

[114] **Westminster Abbey Muniment Room and Library**
London SW1P 3PA

Tel 071–222 5152 ext 228
Fax 071–233 2072

Keeper of the Muniments:
R Mortimer

● M–F 10–1 2–4.45
Photographs
P

[115] **Westminster Diocesan Archives**
16A Abingdon Road, Kensington,
London W8 6AF

Tel 071–938 3580

Archivist: Revd I Dickie

● T–F 10–1 2–5

[116] **Dr Williams's Library**
14 Gordon Square, London WC1H
0AG

Tel 071–387 3727

Librarian: JO Creasey

● M, W, F 10–5, T, Th 10–6.30.
Closed first two weeks in August

GREATER MANCHESTER

[117] **Greater Manchester County Record Office**
56 Marshall Street, New Cross,
Manchester M4 5FU

Tel 061–832 5284
Fax 061–839 3808

County Archivist: Miss M Patch

M 1–5, T–F 9–5, second and
fourth S in month 9–4
Readers ticket
Photographs Microfilm Repair★
P

CA Wright, *Summary of collections*,
2nd edn, 1988

[118] **Bolton Archive Service**
Central Library, Civic Centre, Le
Mans Crescent, Bolton BL1 1SE

Tel 0204 22311 ext 2179
Fax 0204 363224

Borough Archivist: TK Campbell

T, Th 9.30–7.30, W 9.30–1,
F, S 9.30–5
Photographs
P

Guide to the Bolton Archive Service,
1988

[119] **Bury Archive Service**
Derby Hall Annexe, Edwin Street,
Bury BL9 0AS

Tel 061–797 6697

Archivist: KJ Mulley

● T–F 10–1 2–5

[120] **Manchester Central Library, Local Studies Unit**
St Peter's Square,
Manchester M2 5PD

Tel 061–234 1979/1980

Archivist: Miss JM Ayton

M–W, F 10–8, S 10–12 1–5
Photographs Microfilm Repair
P M&T D (Manchester)

[121] **Rochdale Libraries, Local Studies Department**
Area Central Library, Esplanade,
Rochdale OL16 1AQ

Tel 0706 514915

Local Studies Librarian:
Mrs J Higson

M, Th 9.30–7.30, T, F 9.30–5.30,
W 9.30–5, S 9.30–4
Photographs Microfilm

[122] **Salford Archives Centre**
658–662 Liverpool Road, Irlam,
Manchester M30 5AD

Tel 061–775 5643

City Archivist: AN Cross

● M–F 9–4.30
P

[123] **Stockport Archive Service**
Central Library, Wellington Road
South, Stockport SK1 3RS

Tel 061–474 4534
Fax 061–474 7750

Archivist: Mrs MJ Myerscough

● M–F 9–8, S 9–4
Photographs
P

MJ Critchlow, *Guide to archive calendars 1–14*, 1982

[124] **Tameside Archive Service**
Tameside Local Studies Library,
Astley Cheetham Public Library,
Trinity Street, Stalybridge
SK15 2BN

Tel 061–338 2708/3831

Archivist: Gillian Cooke

M–W, F 9–7.30, S 9–4
Photographs
P

[125] **Wigan Archives Service**
Wigan Record Office, Town Hall,
Leigh WN7 2DY

Tel 0942 672421 ext 266

Heritage Officer: AD Gillies
Archivist: NP Webb

● M, T, Th, F 10–1 2–4.30
Photographs Microfilm Repair
P M&T D (Liverpool: parish records of Wigan and Winwick deaneries)

[126] **John Rylands University Library of Manchester**
Deansgate, Manchester M3 3EH

Tel 061–834 5343
Fax 061–273 7488

Administrator: P McNiven

● M–F 10–5.30, S 10–1
Readers ticket. Letter of introduction
Photographs Microfilm Repair
M&T

Methodist Archives and Research Centre

Tel 061–834 5343

Methodist Church Archivist:
G Lloyd

● M–F 10–5.30, S 10–1

[127] **National Museum of Labour History**
103 Princess Street,
Manchester M1 6DD

Tel 061–228 7212

Director: N Mansfield
Archivist: S Bird

● M–F 10–5

MERSEYSIDE

[128] **National Museums and Galleries on Merseyside, Maritime Records Centre**
Merseyside Maritime Museum,
Albert Dock, Liverpool L3 4AA

Tel 051–207 0001 ext 418
Fax 051–709 3003

Curator of Archives: JG Read

T–Th 10.30–4.30
Admission fee
Photographs Repair
P

[129] **Merseyside Record Office**
Cunard Building (4th Floor), Pier Head, Liverpool L3 1EG

Tel 051–236 8038
Fax 051–207 1342

Archivist in charge: Margaret Procter

● M–F 9.15–4.45
P

[130] **Liverpool Record Office and Local History Department**
City Libraries, William Brown Street, Liverpool L3 8EW

Tel 051–225 5417
Fax 051–207 1342

Principal Archives Officer:
Miss J Smith

M–Th 9–7.30, F, S 9–5
Readers ticket
Photographs Microfilm Repair
P M&T D (Liverpool)

[131] **St Helens Local History and Archives Library**
Central Library, Gamble Institute, Victoria Square, St Helens WA10 1DY

Tel 0744 24061 ext 2952
Fax 0744 20836

Local History Librarian and Archivist: Mrs VL Hainsworth

M, W 9.30–8, T, Th–S 9.30–5
Photographs

[132] **Wirral Archives Service**
Birkenhead Reference Library,
Borough Road, Birkenhead
L41 2XB

Tel 051–652 6106/7/8
Fax 051–653 7320

Archivist: DN Thompson

● M, T, Th, F 10–8, S 10–1 2–5
Photographs
P

[133] **Liverpool University, Sydney Jones Library**
PO Box 123, Liverpool L69 3DA

Tel 051–794 2696

Curator of Special Collections:
Ms K Hooper

● M–F 9–5

A guide to the manuscript collections in Liverpool University Library, 1962

[134] **Liverpool University Archives Unit**
PO Box 147, Liverpool L69 3BX

Tel 051–794 5424
Fax 051–708 6502

University Archivist: MG Cook

M–F 9.30–5
Photographs

[135] Birmingham Central Library, Archives Division
Chamberlain Square, Birmingham
B3 3HQ

Tel 021–235 4217
Fax 021–233 4458

Principal Archivist: NW Kingsley

M, T, Th–S 9–5
Readers ticket
Photographs Repair
P M&T D (Birmingham)

[136] Coventry City Record Office
Mandela House, Bayley Lane,
Coventry CV1 5RG

Tel 0203 832418/832414

City Archivist: DJ Rimmer

● M–Th 8.45–4.45, F 8.45–4.15
Photographs Repair
P M&T

[137] Dudley Archives and Local History Service
Mount Pleasant Street,
Coseley, Dudley WV14 9JR

Tel 0902 880011

Archivist: Mrs KH Atkins

● T, W, F 9–5, Th 9–7, first and
third S in month 9.30–12.30
Photographs Microfilm
P D (Lichfield, Worcester: Dudley
parish records)

[138] Sandwell District Libraries
Local Studies Centre, Smethwick
Library, High Street, Smethwick,
Warley B66 1AB

Tel 021–558 2561

Borough Archivist:
Miss CM Harrington

● M, F 9–7, T, W 9–6, Th, S 9–1
Microfilm
P D (Birmingham: Warley
deanery)

[139] Walsall Archives Service
Local History Centre, Essex Street,
Walsall WS2 7AS

Tel 0922 721305/6

Archivist/Local Studies Officer:
R Bond

T, Th 9.30–5.30, W 9.30–7,
F 9.30–5, S 9.30–1
Photographs Microfilm Repair
P M&T

[140] Wolverhampton Borough Archives
Central Library, Snow Hill,
Wolverhampton WV1 3AX

Tel 0902 312025 ext 137
Fax 0902 714579

Borough Archivist: Miss EA Rees

● M–S 10–1 2–5 (W, S by
arrangement)
Photographs Repair
P

[141] Birmingham University Library, Special Collections Department
Edgbaston, Birmingham B15 2TT

Tel 021–414 5838
Fax 021–471 4691

Sub-Librarian (Special Collections):
BS Benedikz

● M–F 9–5.15 (to 5 in vacations).
Closed second week in July
Photographs Microfilm Repair★
P

CL Penney, 'The manuscript
collections of the University of
Birmingham Library', *Archives*,
xvii, 1986

[142] **Warwick University Modern Records Centre**
University Library, Coventry
CV4 7AL

Tel 0203 524219

Archivist: RA Storey

● M–Th 9–1 1.30–5, F 9–1 1.30–4.
Closed one week at Easter, ten
days at Christmas
Repair

RA Storey and A Tough,
*Consolidated guide to the Modern
Records Centre*, 1986

NORFOLK

[143] **Norfolk Record Office**
Central Library, Norwich
NR2 1NJ

Tel 0603 761349

County Archivist:
Miss JM Kennedy

● M–F 9–5, S 9–12
Readers ticket
Photographs Microfilm Repair★
P M&T D (Norwich. Ely: parish
records of Feltwell and Fincham
deaneries)

NORTHAMPTONSHIRE

[144] **Northamptonshire Record Office**
Wootton Hall Park, Northampton
NN4 9BQ

Tel 0604 762129
Fax 0604 767562

County Archivist: Miss R Watson

● M–W 9–4.45, Th 9–7.45,
F 9–4.30, two S each month
Photographs Microfilm Repair
P M&T D (Peterborough)

NORTHUMBERLAND

[145] **Northumberland Record Office**
Melton Park, North Gosforth,
Newcastle upon Tyne NE3 5QX

Tel 091–236 2680

County Archivist: Mrs AM Burton

M 9–9, T–Th 9–5, F 9–4.30
Photographs
P M&T D (Newcastle)

*Northumberland records: a guide to the
collections in the Northumberland
Record Office* (in progress)

[146] **Berwick upon Tweed Record Office**
Council Offices, Wallace Green,
Berwick upon Tweed TD15 1ED

Tel 0289 330044 ext 275
Fax 0289 330540

Archivist in charge:
Mrs LA Bankier

W, Th 9.30–1 2–5
P

NOTTINGHAMSHIRE

[147] **Nottinghamshire Archives Office**
County House, High Pavement,
Nottingham NG1 1HR

Tel 0602 504524

Principal Archivist: AJM Henstock

M, W–F 9–4.45, T 9–7.15,
S 9–12.15
Readers ticket
Repair
P M&T D (Southwell)

PA Kennedy, *Guide to the
Nottinghamshire County Records
Office*, 1960

The office will move to new
premises in Castle Meadow Road,
Nottingham early in 1993

[148] **British Geological Survey Library**
Keyworth, Nottingham
NG12 5GG

Tel 06077 6111 ext 3205
Fax 06077 6602

Chief Librarian and Archivist:
G McKenna

M–Th 9–5, F 9–4.30
Photographs Microfilm
P

[149] **Nottingham University Library, Manuscripts Department**
Hallward Library, University
Park, Nottingham NG7 2RD

Tel 0602 484848 ext 3440
Fax 0602 420825

Keeper of the Manuscripts:
Dorothy B Johnston

● M–F 9–5
Photographs Microfilm Repair
P M&T

OXFORDSHIRE

[150] **Oxfordshire Archives**
County Hall, New Road, Oxford
OX1 1ND

Tel 0865 815203
Fax 0865 810187

Principal Archivist: C Boardman

● M–Th 8.45–5, F 10–4
Readers ticket
Microfilm Repair
P M&T D (Oxford)

Oxfordshire County Record Office and its records, 1938. *Summary catalogue of the privately-deposited records in the Oxfordshire County Record Office*, 1966

[151] **Bodleian Library, Department of Western Manuscripts**
Broad Street, Oxford OX1 3BG

Tel 0865 277152
Fax 0865 277182

Keeper of Western Manuscripts:
Mrs M Clapinson

Term: M–F 9–10, Vacation: M–F
9–7, S 9–1 all year. Closed week
following August bank holiday
Readers ticket. Letter of
introduction. Admission fee
Photographs Microfilm Repair
M&T

Summary catalogue of western manuscripts in the Bodleian Library . . ., 7 vols, 1895–1953, reprinted 1980

Rhodes House Library
South Parks Road, Oxford
OX1 3RG

Tel 0865 270909
Fax 0865 277182

Librarian: AS Bell

● Term: M–F 9–7, Vacation:
M–F 9–5, S 9–1 all year
Readers ticket. Letter of
introduction. Admission fee
Photographs Microfilm Repair

LB Frewer and WS Byrne,
Manuscript collections . . ., 4 vols,
1968–78

[152] **Nuffield College Library**
Oxford OX1 1NF

Tel 0865 278550
Fax 0865 278621

Archivist: R Temple

● M–F 9.30–1 2–6, S 9.30–1.
Closed in August
Letter of introduction

[153] **Pusey House Library**
Pusey House, 61 St Giles, Oxford
OX1 3LZ

Tel 0865 278415

Custodian: Revd HR Smythe

● M–F 9.15–12.15 2–4.45,
S 9.15–12.15. Closed during part
of long vacation
Readers ticket. Letter of
introduction. Admission fee

[154] **Regents Park College,
Angus Library**
Pusey Street, Oxford OX1 2LB

Tel 0865 59887

Librarian/Archivist: Mrs SJ Mills

● M–F 9.30–4. Closed two weeks
at Christmas and Easter and most
of August
Letter of introduction. Admission
fee (genealogical researchers)

[155] **St Antony's College,
Middle East Centre**
Oxford OX2 6JF

Tel 0865 59651 ext 264

Fellow in charge: D Hopwood

Address correspondence to the
Librarian

● T, W 9.30–12.45, 1.45–5.
Closed four weeks in summer and
two weeks at Christmas and Easter
Letter of introduction
Photographs

D Grimwood-Jones, *Sources for the
history of the British in the Middle
East 1800–1978. A catalogue of the
private papers collection . . .*, 1979

SHROPSHIRE

[156] **Shropshire Records and
Research Unit, Shropshire
Record Office**
Shirehall, Abbey Foregate,
Shrewsbury SY2 6ND

Tel 0743 252852
Fax 0743 60315

Head of Records and Research:
Miss RE Bagley

● M, T, Th 9.30–12.40 1.20–5,
F 9.30–12.40 1.20–4. Closed two
weeks in late autumn
Photographs Repair
P M&T D (Hereford: parish
records of Ludlow archdeaconry.
Lichfield: parish records of Salop
archdeaconry)

[157] **Shropshire Records and
Research Unit, Local Studies
Library**
Castle Gates, Shrewsbury SY1 2AS

Tel 0743 361058

Deputy Head of Records and
Research: AM Carr

● M, W, S 9.30–12.30 1.30–5,
T, F 9.30–12.30 1.30–7.30
Photographs
M&T D (Hereford: parish records
of Ludlow archdeaconry. Lichfield:
parish records of Salop
archdeaconry)

SOMERSET

[158] **Somerset Archive and
Record Service**
Obridge Road, Taunton TA2 7PU

Tel 0823 278805/337600
(appointments)

County Archivist: JAS Green

● T–Th 9–4.50, F 9–4.20,
S 9.15–12.15
Photographs Microfilm Repair★
P M&T D (Bath and Wells)

STAFFORDSHIRE

[159] Staffordshire Record Office
County Buildings, Eastgate Street, Stafford ST16 2LZ

Tel 0785 223121 ext 8380/8373

County Archivist: DV Fowkes

● M–Th 9–1 1.30–5, F 9–1
1.30–4.30, S 9–12.30
Readers ticket
Repair
P M&T D (Lichfield: parish
records of Stafford archdeaconry)

[160] William Salt Library
Eastgate Street, Stafford ST16 2LZ

Tel 0785 52276

Librarian: DV Fowkes

T–Th 9–1 2–5, F 9–1 2–4.30,
second and fourth S in month
9.30–1
M&T

[161] Lichfield Joint Record Office
Lichfield Library, The Friary,
Lichfield WS13 6QG

Tel 0543 256787

Principal Area Librarian
(genealogical enquiries): Miss
EM Hughes
Archivist (historical enquiries): Mrs
J Hampartumian

● M, T, Th, F 10–5.15,
W 10–4.30
Readers ticket
Repair
P M&T D (Lichfield)

[162] Keele University Library
Keele ST5 5BG

Tel 0782 621111 ext 3741
Fax 0782 613847

Archives and Special Collections:
M Phillips, Miss M Greive

● M–F 9.30–5. Closed ten days at
Easter and August bank holiday
Readers ticket
Photographs Microfilm

SUFFOLK

[163] Suffolk Record Office, Ipswich Branch
Gatacre Road, Ipswich IP1 2LQ

Tel 0473 264541

Archives Service Manager: Miss
RA Rogers
Branch Archivist: DR Jones

● M–Th 9–5, F 9–4, S 9–1 2–5
Readers ticket
Photographs Microfilm Repair★
P M&T D (St Edmundsbury and
Ipswich: Ipswich and Suffolk
archdeaconries)

[164] Suffolk Record Office, Bury St Edmunds Branch
Raingate Street, Bury St Edmunds
IP33 1RX

Tel 0284 722522

Branch Archivist: RG Thomas

M–Th 9–5, F 9–4, S 9–1 2–5
Readers ticket
Photographs Microfilm Repair★
P M&T D (St Edmundsbury and
Ipswich: Sudbury archdeaconry,
Hadleigh deanery)

[165] Suffolk Record Office, Lowestoft Branch
Central Library, Clapham Road,
Lowestoft NR32 1DR

Tel 0502 566325 ext 3308
Fax 0502 512199

Branch Archivist: Miss K Chantry

M–Th, S 9.15–5, F 9.15–6
Readers ticket
Repair★
P D (St Edmundsbury and
Ipswich: NE Suffolk parish
records)

SURREY

[166] Surrey Record Office
County Hall, Penrhyn Road,
Kingston upon Thames KT1 2DN

Tel 081–541 9065
Fax 081–541 9005

County Archivist: DB Robinson

M–W, F 9.30–4.45, S 9.30–12.30
by appointment
Repair
P M&T D (Southwark: parish
records. Guildford: parish records
of Emly and Epsom deaneries)

The records in Kingston Heritage
Centre are made available in the
searchroom, by appointment
Tel 081–541 9064

Borough Archivist:
Mrs A McCormack

*Guide to the Kingston borough
archives*, 1971

**[167] Surrey Record Office,
Guildford Muniment Room**
Castle Arch, Guildford GU1 3SX

Tel 0483 573942

Archivist in charge:
Mrs SJ Himsworth

● T–F 9.30–12.30 1.45–4.45, first
and third S mornings in month by
arrangement
P M&T D (Guildford: parish ·
records, except deaneries of Emly
and Epsom)

*Summary guide to Guildford Muniment
Room*, 1967

EAST SUSSEX

[168] East Sussex Record Office
The Maltings, Castle Precincts,
Lewes BN7 1YT

Tel 0273 482349
Fax 0273 473321

County Archivist: CR Davey

● M–Th 8.45–4.45, F 8.45–4.15
Readers ticket
Microfilm Repair
P D (Chichester: East Sussex
parish records)

JA Brent, *East Sussex Record Office:
a short guide*, 1988

[169] Sussex University Library
Falmer, Brighton BN1 9QL

Tel 0273 678157

Librarian: AN Peasgood

● M–Th 9–1 2–5
Photographs

WEST SUSSEX

[170] West Sussex Record Office
Sherburne House, 3 Orchard
Street, Chichester

Tel 0243 533911
Fax 0243 777952

County Archivist: Mrs P Gill

M–F 9.15–4.45. Closed second full
week in December
Readers ticket
Photographs Microfilm Repair
P M&T D (Chichester)

Address correspondence to County
Hall, Chichester PO19 1RN

TYNE AND WEAR

**[171] Tyne and Wear Archives
Service**
Blandford House, Blandford
Square, Newcastle upon Tyne
NE1 4JA

Tel 091–232 6789

Chief Archivist: B Jackson

M, W–F 8.45–5.15, T 8.45–8.30
Photographs Microfilm Repair★
P M&T

[172] **Gateshead Central Library, Local Studies Collection**
Prince Consort Road, Gateshead NE8 4LN

Tel 091–477 3478

Local Studies Librarian: TS Marshall

M, T, Th, F 9.30–7.30, W 9.30–5, S 9.30–1
Photographs
M&T

FWD Manders, *Gateshead archives: a guide*, 1968

[173] **Newcastle upon Tyne University, Robinson Library**
Newcastle upon Tyne NE2 4HQ

Tel 091–222 7671/7656
Fax 091–261 1182

Special Collections Librarians: Lesley Gordon, RS Firth

● M–F 9.15–5
Letter of introduction
Photographs Repair★

WARWICKSHIRE

[174] **Warwickshire County Record Office**
Priory Park, Cape Road, Warwick CV34 4JS

Tel 0926 412735
Fax 0926 412471

County Archivist: C Jeens

T–Th 9–1 2–5.30, F 9–1 2–5, S 9–12.30
Readers ticket
Photographs Microfilm Repair
P M&T D (Coventry. Birmingham: parish records)

[175] **Shakespeare Birthplace Trust Records Office**
Shakespeare Centre, Stratford-upon-Avon CV37 6QW

Tel 0789 204016
Fax 0789 296083

Senior Archivist: R Bearman

M–F 9.30–1 2–5, S 9.30–12.30
Photographs Repair
P M&T D (Coventry: parish records of Stratford-upon-Avon and Shottery)

ISLE OF WIGHT

[176] **Isle of Wight County Record Office**
26 Hillside, Newport PO30 2EB

Tel 0983 823831/821000 ext 3820/1

County Archivist: CD Webster

● M–Th 9–1 2–5.30, F 9–1 2–5
Readers ticket
Photographs
P M&T D (Portsmouth: parish records of Isle of Wight archdeaconry)

WILTSHIRE

[177] **Wiltshire Record Office**
County Hall, Trowbridge BA14 8JG

Tel 0225 753641
Fax 0225 765196

County Archivist: SD Hobbs

M–F 9–5, second and fourth W in month 9–8.30
Readers ticket
Photographs Microfilm Repair
P M&T D (Salisbury. Bristol: parish records of Swindon archdeaconry)

NORTH YORKSHIRE

[178] **National Railway Museum Reading Room**
Leeman Road, York YO2 4XJ

Tel 0904 621261
Fax 0904 611112

Curator, Information Services:
Ms C Heap
Curator, Archive and Pictorial
Collections: R Durack

● M–F 10.30–5
Readers ticket
Photographs

[179] **North Yorkshire County Record Office**
Malpas Road, Northallerton
DL7 8TB

Tel 0609 777585
Fax 0609 780447

County Archivist: MY Ashcroft

Address correspondence to County
Hall, Northallerton DL7 8AF

● M, T, Th 9–4.50, W 9–8.50,
F 9–4.20
Microfilm Repair
D (Bradford, Ripon, York: parish
records)

[180] **York City Archives Department**
Art Gallery Building, Exhibition
Square, York YO1 2EW

Tel 0904 651533

City Archivist: Mrs RJ Freedman

T–Th 9.30–12.30 2–5.30, M, F by
appointment only
Photographs Microfilm Repair
P

*Brief guide to York City Archives
Department collections*, 1986

[181] **York University, Borthwick Institute of Historical Research**
St Anthony's Hall, York
YO1 2PW

Tel 0904 642315

Director: DM Smith

● M–F 9.30–12.50, 2–4.50. Closed
one week at Easter and part of
Christmas vacation
Photographs Microfilm Repair★
P M&T D (York)

DM Smith, *A guide to the archive
collections in the Borthwick Institute of
Historical Research*, 1973,
Supplement, 1980

[182] **York Minster Archives**
York Minster Library, Dean's
Park, York YO1 2JD

Tel 0904 625308
Fax 0904 654604

Archivist: MS Dorrington

● M–F 9–5
Photographs Microfilm Repair
P

KM Longley, *Guide to the archives
and manuscript collections in York
Minster Library*, 1977

SOUTH YORKSHIRE

[183] **Barnsley Archive Service**
Central Library, Shambles Street,
Barnsley S70 2JF

Tel 0226 733241
Fax 0226 285458

Archivist: Miss RF Vyse

M–W 9.30–1 2–6, F 9.30–1 2–5,
S 9.30–1
Photographs Repair

[184] **Doncaster Archives Department**
King Edward Road, Balby,
Doncaster DN4 0NA

Tel 0302 859811

Archivist: BJ Barber

M–F 9–12.30 2–5
P M&T D (Sheffield: Doncaster archdeaconry)

Guide to the Archives Department,
1981

[185] **Rotherham Metropolitan Borough Archives and Local Studies Section**
Brian O'Malley Central Library,
Walker Place, Rotherham S65 1JH

Tel 0709 823616/382121 ext 3616
Fax 0709 823650

Archivist: AP Munford

M–W, F 10–5, Th 1–7, S 9–5
Photographs
P

[186] **Sheffield Archives**
52 Shoreham Street, Sheffield
S1 4SP

Tel 0742 734756
Fax 0742 735009

Principal Archivist: R Childs

● M–Th 9.30–5.30, S 9–4.30
Readers ticket
Photographs Microfilm Repair★
P M&T D (Sheffield)

R Meredith, *Guide to the manuscript collections in the Sheffield City Libraries,* 1956, *Supplement (accessions 1956–76),* 1976

[187] **Sheffield University Library**
Western Bank, Sheffield S10 2TN

Tel 0742 768555 ext 4334/4343
Fax 0742 739826

Archivist: PW Carnell

● Term: M–Th 9–9.30, F 9–5,
S 9–1, Vacation: M–F 9–5,
S 9–12.30
Readers ticket
Photographs Microfilm

WEST YORKSHIRE

[188] **West Yorkshire Archive Service, Wakefield Headquarters**
Registry of Deeds, Newstead
Road, Wakefield WF1 2DE

Tel 0924 295982

Archivist to the Joint Committee:
RL Frost
Principal Archivist: PM Bottomley

M 9–8, T–Th 9–5, F 9–1. Closed
one week in February
Microfilm (for whole of West
Yorkshire Archive Service)
Repair★
P M&T D (Wakefield)

[189] **West Yorkshire Archive Service, Bradford**
15 Canal Road, Bradford
BD1 4AT

Tel 0274 731931

District Archivist: D James

● M–W 9.30–1 2–5, Th 9.30–1
2–8, F 9.30–1. Closed one week in
February
Repair★
P D (Bradford)

[190] **West Yorkshire Archive Service, Calderdale**
Central Library, Northgate House,
Northgate, Halifax HX1 1UN

Tel 0422 357257 ext 2636
Fax 0422 349458

District Archivist: A Betteridge

● M, T, Th, F 10–5.30, W 10–12
by arrangement. Closed one week
in February
Repair★
P D (Bradford: parish records)

*Calderdale Archives 1964–1989: an
illustrated guide to Calderdale District
Archives*

[191] **West Yorkshire Archive
Service, Kirklees**
Central Library, Princess
Alexandra Walk, Huddersfield
HD1 2SU

Tel 0484 513808 ext 207

District Archivist: Miss J Burhouse

● M, T, Th 9–8, W 9.30–5,
F 9–4, S 9–4 by arrangement only.
Closed one week in February
Photographs Repair★
P M&T

*Kirklees Archives 1959–1989: an
illustrated guide to Kirklees District
Archives*

[192] **West Yorkshire Archive
Service, Leeds**
Chapeltown Road, Sheepscar,
Leeds LS7 3AP

Tel 0532 628339

District Archivist: WJ Connor

● M–F 9.30–5. Closed one week
in February
Repair★
P M&T D (Ripon. Bradford:
parish records)

*Leeds Archives 1938–1988: an
illustrated guide to Leeds District
Archives*

[193] **West Yorkshire Archive
Service, Yorkshire
Archaeological Society**
Claremont, 23 Clarendon Road,
Leeds LS2 9NZ

Tel 0532 456362

Archivist in charge: Mrs S Thomas

T, W 2–8.30, Th, F 9.30–5,
S 9.30–5 by appointment
Repair★
M&T

EW Crossley, *Catalogue of
manuscripts and deeds in the library of
Yorkshire Archaeological Society*, 1931,
reprinted 1986. S Thomas, *Guide to
the archives of the Yorkshire
Archaeological Society 1931–83 and to
collections deposited with the Society*,
1985

[194] **Leeds University Libraries**
Leeds, LS2 9JT

University Librarian and Keeper of
the Brotherton Collection: RP Carr

Brotherton Collection

Tel 0532 335518
Fax 0532 334381

Sub-Librarian, Brotherton
Collection: CDW Sheppard

● M–F 9–1 2.15–5
Letter of introduction
Photographs Microfilm

*The Brotherton Collection, University
of Leeds; its contents described . . .*,
1986

Brotherton Library,
Department of Manuscripts and
Special Collections

Tel 0532 335526

Sub-Librarian: PS Morrish

M–F 9–5
Letter of introduction
Photographs Microfilm

Edward Boyle Library,
Liddle Collection

Tel 0532 335566

Keeper: PH Liddle

By appointment only
Photographs Microfilm

WALES

CLWYD

[195] Clwyd Record Office, Hawarden Branch
The Old Rectory, Hawarden,
Deeside CH5 3NR

Tel 0244 532364
Fax 0244 538344

County Archivist: AG Veysey

M–Th 9–4.45, F 9–4.15
Readers ticket
Photographs Repair★
P M&T D (St Asaph: parish
records)

Administrative assistance to St
Deiniol's Library, Hawarden

AG Veysey, *Guide to the Flintshire
Record Office*, 1974

[196] Clwyd Record Office, Ruthin Branch
46 Clwyd Street, Ruthin
LL15 1HP

Tel 08242 3077

Senior Archivist: RK Matthias

M–Th 9–4.45, F 9–4.15
Readers ticket
Photographs Repair★
P M&T D (St Asaph: parish
records)

DYFED

[197] National Library of Wales, Department of Manuscripts and Records
Aberystwyth SY23 3BU

Tel 0970 623816
Fax 0970 615709

Keeper of Manuscripts and
Records: G Jenkins

M–F 9.30–6, S 9.30–5. Closed first
full week in October
Readers ticket
Photographs Microfilm Repair
P M&T D (Province of Wales)

Catalogue of manuscripts, vol I, 1921.
*Handlist of manuscripts in the National
Library of Wales,* vols I–IV, 1940–86

[198] Dyfed Archives Service, Carmarthenshire Area Record Office
County Hall, Carmarthen
SA31 1JP

Tel 0267 233333 ext 4182

County Archivist: J Owen

M 9–7, T–Th 9–4.45, F 9–4.15,
first and third S in month
9.30–12.30 by appointment
P M&T D (St Davids: parish
records)

S Beckley, *Carmarthenshire Record
Office: a survey of archive holdings,*
1980

[199] **Dyfed Archives Service, Cardiganshire Area Record Office**
County Office, Marine Terrace, Aberystwyth SY23 2DE

Tel 0970 617581 ext 2120

Assistant Archivist: Janet Marx

T, Th 9–1 2–4.45
P M&T D (St Davids: parish records)

[200] **Dyfed Archives Service, Pembrokeshire Area Record Office**
The Castle, Haverfordwest SA61 2EF

Tel 0437 763707

Archivist in charge: C Hughes

M–Th 9–4.45, F 9–4.15, first and third S in month 9.30–12.30
Repair
P M&T D (St Davids: parish records)

MID AND SOUTH GLAMORGAN

[201] **Glamorgan Record Office**
County Hall, Cathays Park, Cardiff CF1 3NE

Tel 0222 780282
Fax 0222 780027

Glamorgan Archivist:
Mrs P Moore

● T–Th 9–5, F 9–4.30
Photographs Repair★
P M&T D (Llandaff, Swansea and Brecon: parish records)

WEST GLAMORGAN

[202] **West Glamorgan Record Office**
County Hall, Oystermouth Road, Swansea SA1 3SN

Tel 0792 471589
Fax 0792 471340

County Archivist:
Miss SG Beckley

● M–Th 9–5 (M 5.30–7.30 by arrangement)
P M&T D (Swansea and Brecon: parish records)

[203] **University College of Swansea Library**
Singleton Park, Swansea SA2 8PP

Tel 0792 205678 ext 4042

Archivist: DA Bevan

● M–F 9–5
Photographs Microfilm

GWENT

[204] **Gwent County Record Office**
County Hall, Cwmbran NP44 2XH

Tel 0633 832266/832217
Fax 0633 838225

County Archivist: D Tibbott

T–Th 9.30–5, F 9.30–4
Readers ticket
Photographs Microfilm Repair
P M&T D (Monmouth, Swansea and Brecon: parish records)

WH Baker, *Guide to the Monmouthshire Record Office*, 1959

GWYNEDD

[205] Gwynedd Archives and Museums Service, Caernarfon Area Record Office
Victoria Dock, Caernarfon

Tel 0286 679095
Fax 0286 679637

County Archivist and Museums
Officer: BR Parry
Area Archivist: G Haulfryn
Williams
Address correspondence to County
Offices, Shirehall Street,
Caernarfon LL55 1SH

M, T, Th, F 9.30–12.30 1.30–5,
W 9.30–12.30 1.30–7. Closed
second full week in October
Readers ticket
Photography Repair*
P M&T D (Bangor.St Asaph:
parish records)

WO Williams, *Guide to the
Caernarvonshire Record Office, 1952*

[206] Gwynedd Archives and Museums Service, Dolgellau Area Record Office
Cae Penarlag, Dolgellau LL40 2YB

Tel 0341 422341 ext 261

Area Archivist and Museum
Officer: Miss A Rhydderch

M–F 9.15–1 1.55–4.45. Closed first
full week in November
Readers ticket
Photographs Repair
P M&T

[207] Gwynedd Archives and Museums Service, Llangefni Area Record Office
Shire Hall, Llangefni LL77 7TW

Tel 0248 750262 ext 269

Area Archivist: EW Thomas

M–F 9–5. Closed first full week in
November
Readers ticket
Photographs
P M&T D (Bangor: Anglesey
parish records)

[208] University College of North Wales, Department of Manuscripts
Bangor LL57 2DG

Tel 0248 351151 ext 2966
Fax 0248 370576

Archivist and Keeper of
Manuscripts: T Roberts

M–F 9–1 2–5, W to 9 in term
Repair
P M&T

POWYS

[209] Powys County Archives Office
County Hall, Llandrindod Wells
LD1 5LD

Tel 0597 826087/8

Archivist: G Reid

● M–Th 9–12.30 1.30–5,
F 9–12.30 1.30–4
P

SCOTLAND

BORDERS

[210] Borders Region Archive and Local History Centre
Regional Library Headquarters, St Mary's Mill, Selkirk TD7 5EW

Tel 0750 20842
Fax 0750 22875

Principal Librarian/Archivist: Miss R Brown

● M–Th 8.45–1 2–5, F 8.45–1 2–4
P(S)

CENTRAL

[211] Central Regional Council Archives Department
Unit 6, Burghmuir Industrial Estate, Stirling FK7 7PY

Tel 0786 50745

Regional Archivist: GA Dixon

M–F 9–5
Photographs
P(S)

DUMFRIES & GALLOWAY

[212] Dumfries and Galloway Regional Library Service
Ewart Public Library, Catherine Street, Dumfries DG1 1JB

Tel 0387 53820
Fax 0387 60294

Reference and Local Collection Librarian: G Roberts

● M–W, F 10–7.30, Th, S 10–5
Photographs
P(S)

[213] Dumfries Archive Centre ✳
33 Burns Street, Dumfries DG1 2PS

Tel 0387 69254
Fax 0387 67225

Archivist: Miss MM Stewart

● T, W, F 11–1 2–5, Th 6–9

FIFE

[214] St Andrews University Library
North Street, St Andrews KY16 9TR

Tel 0334 76161 ext 514
Fax 0334 75851

Keeper of Manuscripts: RN Smart

M–F 9–12 2–5, S 9–12 term only
Photographs Microfilm Repair★
P(S)

GRAMPIAN

[215] Grampian Regional Archives
Old Aberdeen House, Dunbar Street, Aberdeen AB2 1UE

Tel 0224 481775

Regional Archivist: Mrs BR Cluer

● M–F 10–1 2–4
Photographs

[216] Moray District Record Office
Tolbooth, High Street, Forres IV36 0AB

Tel 0309 73617
Fax 0309 74166

District Archivist: DA Iredale

M–F 9–12.30 1.30–4.30
Photographs Repair
P(S)

[217] **Aberdeen City Archives**
The Charter Room, The Town
House, Aberdeen AB9 1AQ

Tel 0224 276276 ext 2513
Fax 0224 644364

Archivist: Miss JA Cripps

● M 10.30–12.30 2–4.30,
T–F 9.30–12.30 2–4.30
Photographs
P(S)

[218] **Aberdeen University
Library, Department of Special
Collections and Archives**
King's College, Aberdeen
AB9 2UB

Tel 0224 272598/9
Fax 0224 487048

Head of Special Collections,
University Archivist: CA McLaren

M–F 9.30–4.30
Photographs Microfilm

HIGHLAND

[219] **Highland Regional
Archive**
Inverness Branch Library, Farraline
Park, Inverness IV1 1NH

Tel 0463 220330
Fax 0463 711177

Regional Archivist: RD Steward

Address correspondence to
Kinmylies Buildings, Leachkin
Road, Inverness IV3 6NN

● M–F 9.30–5
Photographs
P(S)

LOTHIAN

[220] **National Library of
Scotland, Department of
Manuscripts**
George IV Bridge, Edinburgh
EH1 1EW

Tel 031–226 4531
Fax 031–226 5620

Keeper of Manuscripts, Maps and
Music: IC Cunningham

M–F 9.30–8.30, S 9.30–1. Closed
first week in October
Readers ticket
Photographs Microfilm Repair

*Summary catalogue of the Advocates
manuscripts, 1971. Catalogue of
manuscripts acquired since 1925,* 6
vols, 1938–86

[221] **Royal Botanic Garden**
The Library, Inverleith Row,
Edinburgh EH3 5LR

Tel 031–552 7171
Fax 031–552 0382

Librarian: CD Will

M–Th 8.30–5, F 8.30–4.30
Photographs

[222] **Scottish Record Office**
HM General Register House,
Edinburgh EH1 3YY

Tel 031–556 6585

Keeper of Records of Scotland:
PM Cadell

M–F 9–4.45. HM General Register
House closed first two weeks and
West Register House third week in
November
Readers ticket
Microfilm Repair★

The National Register of Archives
(Scotland) is maintained at West
Register House, Charlotte Square,
Edinburgh EH2 4DF

M Livingstone, *Guide to the public
records of Scotland deposited in HM
General Register House Edinburgh,*
1905. *List of gifts and deposits in the
Scottish Record Office* vol 1, 1971,
vol 2, 1976

[223] **City of Edinburgh
District Council Archives**
Department of Administration,
City Chambers, High Street,
Edinburgh EH1 1YJ

Tel 031–225 2424 ext 5196
Fax 031–220 1494

City Archivist: AT Wilson

M–Th 9.30–4.30, F 9.30–3.30

[224] Edinburgh University Library, Special Collections Department
George Square, Edinburgh
EH8 9LJ

Tel 031–650 3412/1000
Fax 031–667 9780

Librarian, Special Collections:
JV Howard

● M–F 9–5. Closed second week in August
Readers ticket
Photographs Microfilm Repair

Index to manuscripts, Edinburgh University Library, 2 vols, 1964, *First supplement*, 1981

New College Library,
Mound Place, Edinburgh
EH1 2LU

Tel 031–225 8400 ext 256

● Term: M–Th 9–9, F 9–5.30,
Vacation: M–F 9–5
Readers ticket

Address correspondence to
Edinburgh University Library

[225] Heriot-Watt University Archives
Riccarton, Currie, Edinburgh
EH14 4AS

Tel 031–449 5111 ext 4064

University Archivist: N Reid

● M–F 9.30–4.45 and by arrangement
Photographs

[226] Scottish Catholic Archives
Columba House, 16 Drummond Place, Edinburgh EH3 6PL

Tel 031–556 3661

Keeper: Revd GM Dilworth

By appointment only
Photographs

ORKNEY

[227] Orkney Archives
Orkney Library, Laing Street,
Kirkwall KW15 1NW

Tel 0856 3166 ext 5

Archivist: Miss A Fraser

● M, T, Th, F 9–1 2–4.45. Closed three weeks in mid-February
Readers ticket
Photographs
P(S)

SHETLAND

[228] Shetland Archives
44 King Harald Street, Lerwick
ZE1 0EQ

Tel 0595 3535 ext 269

Archivist: BR Smith

● M–Th 9–1 2–5, F 9–1 2–4
Photographs
P(S)

STRATHCLYDE

[229] Strathclyde Regional Archives
Mitchell Library, North Street,
Glasgow G3 7DN

Tel 041–227 2405

Principal Archivist: AM Jackson

M–Th 9.30–4.45, F 9.30–4
Repair★
P(S)

Ayrshire Subregional Archives
County Buildings, Wellington Square, Ayr KA7 1DR

Tel 041–227 2401/5

Archivist in charge: R Urquhart

● W 10–4
P(S)

Address correspondence to
Strathclyde Regional Archives

[230] **Argyll and Bute District Archives**
Argyll and Bute District Council, Kilmory, Lochgilphead PA31 8RT

Tel 0546 602127 ext 4120
Fax 0546 3956

Archivist: M MacDonald

M–Th 9–5.15, F 9–4
Microfilm

[231] **City of Glasgow, Mitchell Library**
201 North Street, Glasgow
G3 7DN

Tel 041–221 7030 ext 265
Fax 041–204 4824

Acting Departmental Librarian, Rare Books and Manuscripts: HB Whyte

● M–F 9.30–9, S 9.30–5
Photographs Microfilm Repair
P(S)

[232] **Glasgow University Library, Special Collections Department**
Hillhead Street, Glasgow G12 8QE

Tel 041–339 8855 ext 6767
Fax 041–357 5043

Keeper of Special Collections: TD Hobbs

● Term: M–Th 9–9.30, F 9–5, S 9–12.30, Vacation: M–F 9–5, S 9–12.30
Readers ticket
Photographs Microfilm Repair

J Young and PH Aitken, *A catalogue of the manuscripts in the library of the Hunterian Museum . . . ,* 1908

[233] **Glasgow University Archives and Business Record Centre**
The University, Glasgow
G12 8QQ

Tel 041–330 5516
Fax 041–330 4808

University Archivist: MS Moss

● M–F 9.30–4
Readers ticket
Photographs Microfilm Repair
P(S)

[234] **Strathclyde University Archives**
University of Strathclyde, Glasgow G1 1XQ

Tel 041–552 4400 ext 2318

Archivist: JS McGrath

● M–F 9–5
Photographs

[235] **Royal College of Physicians and Surgeons of Glasgow**
234–242 St Vincent Street, Glasgow G2 5RJ

Tel 041–221 6072

Librarian: AM Rodger

● M–F 9.30–5.30

TAYSIDE

[236] **Dundee District Archive and Record Centre**
14 City Square, Dundee DD1 3BY

Tel 0382 23141 ext 4494
Fax 0382 203302

Archivist: IEF Flett

● M–F 9–1 2–5
P(S)

Address correspondence to Administration Division, 21 City Square, Dundee DD1 3BY

[237] **Montrose Public Library**
High Street, Montrose DD10 8PJ

Tel 0674 73256

Local Studies Librarian: Mrs F Scharlau

● M–F 9.30–5, evenings by arrangement
Photographs

[238] **Perth and Kinross District Archive**
Sandeman Library, 16 Kinnoull Street, Perth PH1 5ET

Tel 0738 23329/23320
Fax 0738 36364

Archivist: SJ Connelly

● M–F 9.30–5
P(S)

[239] **Dundee University Library, Archives and Manuscripts Department**
Dundee, Tayside DD1 4HN

Tel 0382 23181 ext 4095
Fax 0382 29190

Archivist: Mrs HJ Auld

● M–W, F 9–5, Th 9–1.30, S morning by appointment (term only)
Photographs Repair*

NORTHERN IRELAND

[240] **Public Record Office of Northern Ireland**
66 Balmoral Avenue, Belfast BT9 6NY

Tel 0232 661621/663286
Fax 0232 665718

Director: APW Malcomson

M–F 9.15–4.45. Closed first two weeks in December
Readers ticket
Photographs Microfilm Repair

THE ISLE OF MAN

[241] **Manx Museum Library**
Kingswood Grove, Douglas, Isle of Man

Tel 0624 675522 ext 133
Fax 0624 661899

Librarian/Archivist:
Miss AM Harrison

M–S 10–5
Photographs Repair
P (Isle of Man) D (Sodor and Man)

THE CHANNEL ISLANDS

GUERNSEY

[242] **States of Guernsey Island Archives Service**
29 Victoria Road, St Peter Port, Guernsey

Tel 0481 724512
Fax 0481 715815

Island Archivist: JH Lenfestey

● M–F 8.30–12.30
P (Guernsey)

Register Offices

[243] Office of Population Censuses and Surveys
St Catherine's House, 10 Kingsway, London WC2B 6JP

Tel 071–242 0262 ext 2446

Director and Registrar General: P Wormold

M–F 8.30–4.30

Has custody of all statutory registers of births, marriages and deaths in England and Wales since 1837

[244] Principal Registry of the Family Division
Somerset House, Strand, London WC2R 1LP

Tel 071–936 6960

Senior Registrar: CF Turner

M–F 10–4.30

Has custody of all wills admitted to probate in England and Wales since 1858

[245] General Register Office (Scotland)
New Register House, Edinburgh EH1 3YT

Tel 031–334 0380

Registrar General: CM Glennie

● M–Th 9.30–4.30, F 9.30–4

Has custody of all statutory registers of births, marriages and deaths in Scotland since 1855 and of all Scottish parish registers earlier than 1855

[246] General Register Office (Northern Ireland)
Oxford House, 49–55 Chichester Street, Belfast BT1 4HL

Tel 0232 235211 ext 2329/2326

Registrar General: R McMurray

M–F 9.30–3.30

Has custody of all statutory registers of births, marriages and deaths in Northern Ireland since 1922

[247] General Registry (Isle of Man)
Finch Road, Douglas, Isle of Man

Tel 0624 673358

Chief Registrar: P Curtis

M–F 9–1 2.15–4.30

Has custody of all statutory registers of births and deaths in the Isle of Man since 1878, marriages since 1883 and records of Church of England baptisms, marriages and burials earlier than these dates. Also maintains the Deeds Registry of wills admitted to probate and deeds since 1910

[248] Greffe (Guernsey)
Royal Court House, Guernsey

Tel 0481 25277

HM Greffier: K Tough

M–F 9–1 2–4

Has custody of the records of the Royal Court, the States of Guernsey, statutory registers of births, marriages and deaths since 1840, wills since 1841, deeds since 1576 and some private collections

List of records in the Greffe, Guernsey, 2 vols, 1969, 1978

[249] Judicial Greffe (Jersey)
States Building, 10 Hill Street, Royal Square, St Helier, Jersey

Tel 0534 75472

Judicial Greffier: BI Le Marguand
Registrar of Deeds: PJ Bisson

M–F 9–1 2–5.15

Has custody of the records of the Royal Court and of the Public Registry of Deeds and the Probate Registry. Also houses the records of the States Assembly and Ecclesiastical Court and the statutory registers of births, marriages and deaths since 1842

Other Useful Addresses

The following organisations may be able to help students to locate specific classes of records

[250] The Royal Commission on Historical Manuscripts

Quality House, Quality Court, Chancery Lane, London WC2A 1HP

Tel 071–242 1198
Fax 071–831 3550

Secretary: CJ Kitching

M–F 9.30–5

Acts as a central clearing-house for information about the nature and location of historical manuscripts and papers outside the public records. The National Register of Archives, the Manorial Documents Register and the Tithe Documents Register are available for public use in its search room. Its publications, which include an annual list of *Accessions to Repositories and Reports added to the National Register of Archives*, are listed in HMSO *History in Print Sectional List 60*, 1990

[251] Army Museums Ogilby Trust

Falklands House, Elmwood Avenue, Feltham, Middlesex TW13 7AA

Tel 081–844 1613/0764 4538/9

Secretary: Colonel PS Walton

● M–F 9.30–5

Acts as a general clearing-house for information about the contents of all regimental and other military museums

[252] British Records Association

18 Padbury Court, London E2 7EH

Tel 071–729 1415

Archivist: Miss SA Snell

Exists to promote and encourage the work of all individuals and institutions interested in the conservation and use of records. Its Records Preservation Section arranges the deposit in appropriate repositories of documents received mainly from the offices of London solicitors

[253] Business Archives Council

185 Tower Bridge Road, London SE1 2UF

Tel 071–407 6110

Provides help in tracing the records of industrial and commercial undertakings, carries out surveys of business archives and offers guidance to companies and institutions on the management of their records

[254] Business Archives Council of Scotland

Glasgow University Archives and Business Records Centre, 13 Thurso Street, Glasgow G11 6PE

Tel 041–339 8855 ext 6494

Surveying Officer: K Wilbraham

Performs similar functions to the Business Archives Council

[255] **Church of England Record Centre**
15 Galleywall Road, South Bermondsey, London SE16 3PB

Tel 071–222 7010
Fax 071–231 5243

Archivist: Mrs BL Hough

M–F 10–5

Acts as a general clearing-house for information on all central records of the Church of England

[256] **Society of Genealogists**
14 Charterhouse Buildings, Goswell Road, London EC1M 7BA

Tel 071–251 8799

Director and Secretary: AJ Camp

T, F, S 10–6, W, Th 10–8. Closed one week in February

Its genealogical reference library is open to non-members on payment of a fee. Holds lists of the names and addresses of regional genealogical societies and of individual professional research workers in this field

Useful Publications

The following publications may be useful to students seeking details of repositories which fall outside the scope of this directory, or of other institutions which may be prepared to make their own records available for research by arrangement

British archives: a guide to archive resources in the United Kingdom, ed J Foster and J Sheppard, 2nd edn, 1989

Directory of Irish archives, ed S Helferty and R Refaussé, 1988

Business Archives Council: directory of corporate archives, compiled by L Richmond and A Turton, 3rd edn, 1992

Capitular libraries and archives in England: a directory of officers and addresses, ed J Williams, 4th edn, 1989

ASLIB Directory of information sources in the United Kingdom, ed EM Codlin, 2 vols, 6th edn, 1990

Directory of British associations, 11th edn, 1992

Museums Association, *Museums Yearbook 1991–92*

Index

P6

JOSEPHINE BARKER (ARCHIVIST)
VESTRY HOUSE MUSEUM
VESTRY ROAD
LONDON E17 9NH
081 509 1917
MON-FRI 10-1 2-5.30

BAPTIST CHURCH (1817AD)
CHURCH SEC MISS IC WITTLE
34 HABGOOD ROAD
LOUGHTON
081 508 3464.

1861 CENSUS

Printed in the United Kingdom by HMSO, Edinburgh
Dd 293665 C13 8/92 (202994)